EUROPA

Moniza Alvi was born in Pakistan and grew up in Hertfordshire. She was co-winner of The Poetry Business Prize in 1991. Her first collection *The Country at My Shoulder* (OUP, 1993) was shortlisted for the T.S. Eliot and Whitbread poetry prizes, and was selected for the New Generation Poets promotion. *A Bowl of Warm Air* (OUP, 1996) was featured in *The Independent on Sunday*'s 'Books of the Year'. *Carrying My Wife* (Bloodaxe Books, 2000) was a Poetry Book Society Recommendation. Her first three collections are reprinted in *Split World: Poems 1990-2005* (Bloodaxe Books, 2008), along with poems from *Souls* (Bloodaxe Books, 2002) and *How the Stone Found Its Voice* (Bloodaxe Books, 2005). Her latest collection, *Europa* (Bloodaxe Books, 2008), is published separately; it is the Poetry Book Society Choice for Summer 2008, and shortlisted for the 2008 T.S. Eliot Prize.

Moniza Alvi reads poems from her first three collections on *The Poetry Quartets 6* (British Council/Bloodaxe Books, 2000), a double-cassette shared with Michael Donaghy, Anne Stevenson and George Szirtes.

She received a Cholmondeley Award in 2002. A book of her poems translated into Dutch was published in Holland by Wagner & Van Santen in 2003.

After a long career as a secondary school teacher, she now lives in south-west London with her husband and young daughter. Moniza Alvi tutors for the the Poetry School and mentors for Exiled Writers Ink. In 2002-04 she was a trainee at the Westminster Pastoral Foundation studying counselling and group analysis. She is a Fellow of the English Association and a trustee of the Poetry Society and of the magazine *Poetry London*.

MONIZA ALVI

Europa

BLOODAXE BOOKS

ISBN: 978 1 85224 803 1

First published 2008 by
Bloodaxe Books Ltd,
Highgreen,
Tarset,
Northumberland NE48 1RP.

www.bloodaxebooks.com
For further information about Bloodaxe titles
please visit our website or write to
the above address for a catalogue.

Bloodaxe Books Ltd acknowledges
the financial assistance of
Arts Council England, North East.

Cover design: Neil Astley & Pamela Robertson-Pearce.

Cover printing: J. Thomson Colour Printers Ltd, Glasgow.

Printed in Great Britain by
Bell & Bain Limited, Glasgow, Scotland.

For Christina Dunhill

ACKNOWLEDGEMENTS

Acknowledgements are due to the editors of the following publications in which some of these poems first appeared: *Alhambra Poetry Calendar 2008* (edited by Shafiq Naz), *The Book of Hopes and Dreams*, ed. Dee Rimbaud (Bluechrome, 2006), *Magma*, *New Writing 15*, ed. Bernardine Evaristo & Maggie Gee (Granta Books, 2007), *Pakistani Literature*, *Poetry London*, *Poetry Review*, *PN Review*, *Pratik* (Nepal) and *Soundings*.

The poem 'Post-Traumatic' was commissioned for *Signs and Humours: The Poetry of Medicine*, ed. Lavinia Greenlaw (Calouste Gulbenkian Foundation, 2007).

I am grateful to the Society of Authors for a bursary awarded in 2007.

Many thanks to all those who gave invaluable assistance with this collection.

CONTENTS

Trauma is a kind of wound. When we call an event *traumatic*, we are borrowing the word from the Greek where it refers to a piercing of the skin, a breaking of the bodily envelope. In physical medicine it denotes damage to tissue.

CAROLINE GARLAND, chapter 'Thinking About Trauma' in *Understanding Trauma*, edited by Caroline Garland (Karnac Books, 1998)

Post-Traumatic

Not now said the mind to the brain
Not yet

And it cloaked itself in amnesia
And time curled up serpent-like –
its dusty mosaics
              cemented together

Time – the cobra
waiting to unleash
              its venom

Not yet, not yet

But under pressure, the mind
started to leak
              vermilion drops

That woman jostling you in a crowd –
you could drive your fist
              like a bus

right through her

Talk to yourself
              Talk to yourself

You don't need to do anything

It's expected
the fuck-offs fired from your mouth
the avalanche
              of words

Until at last you made a clearing
set the house, the plot of land
in some kind of order, little
              by little

Planted a flower
         more open-faced

which now you name
         tentatively –
calm-in-the-storm

love-of-life

Her Symptoms

How easily the knot had come undone
once the time was ripe,
the golden cord falling away
from the wooden chest.

And they all had to be unleashed,
every poisonous one.

In turn
        they forced their way up –

leather-winged, chuckling and hissing
with a devilish fondness for her.

Out they came.
Out, out.
        Swooping,

digging their claws
into her human flesh.
           Until

it seemed there was nothing inside
but the thick lining, a weft in the cloth
that hadn't been there. The lid no longer fitted.
Her jewellery box, but not for jewels.

Almost calm, she could hold it in both hands.

Memory, Memory

Memory, memory,
let off the lead,
run like the wind
through the field
at the back of the house.

And make a kill.

Bring it to me
from undercover,
from the furthest corner.

That scene you proudly
dropped at my feet –
my eyes stayed open
for a second.
Then shut.

Key Words

have become too weighty
   climbed down
from their cardboard thrones
   taken off their paper crowns
    and fled

Words, dread words
   have abdicated
leaving you instead with
   'the thing itself'

So utter the words
   and down you will go
    right down through
     the forest

   through the trapdoor

In Response

The healer, like the lion-tamer,
coaxing the wound
to rise up and perform,
to lie down and die.

The wound responds,
leaping to centre-stage
to dance non-stop
on the mind's thin skin.

Candle

The fresh wound is a candle
lighting steps down into the caves.

Among stalagmites and stalactites
the old wound crouches low.

The Sleeping Wound

Hush, do not waken
the sleeping wound.

It lies on its crimson pillow,
red against red.

The long wound in the afternoon.
The long wound in the evening.

Centuries later,
no longer red,

it opens its eyes
at the most tentative kiss.

So Much More

Fold it away, unfold it
wherever it is – the truth
with its sideways glance,
and so much more up its sleeve.

And seeking its own level
whatever vase it's poured into.

Interior, Degas

We must save this room from itself,
from its wallpaper cage

streaked grey-green,
from the din of its silence,

from the door that takes his weight
as he blocks the keyhole,

from the floor that takes hers,
her half-bare back to him.

This room, closed as a body,
with no visible window.

The rug knows more about it all
than we do.

The oval picture saw part of it
with its dead eye.

The clothes, limp across the bedstead
carry it like smoke.

The mirror can't save the room,
can't draw it in completely:

the woman who couldn't hold herself up
if she wanted to,

the hard-eyed man across the floorboards,
miles from her, in his trousers.

The Beautiful Apology

Light, in proportion to the weightiness
        of the act,
so much lighter than thighs, or genitals,
    lighter than lips.

    The beautiful apology
                        enclosed

in its fine-grained envelope,
trembling like the shut wings
    of a butterfly.

Mermaid
(after Tabitha Vevers)

About human love,
                     she knew nothing.

I'll show you he promised.
But first you need legs.

And he held up
               a knife

with the sharpest of tips
to the ripeness of her emerald tail.

She danced an involuntary dance
captive
              twitching with fear.

Swiftly
          he slit

down the muscular length
exposing the bone in its red canal.

She played dead on the rock

              dead by the blue lagoon
              dead to the ends of her divided tail.

He fell on her, sunk himself deep
into the apex.

Then he fled
               on his human legs.

Human love cried the sea,
the sea in her head.

The Ride

Let me give you a lift,
he said.

And he kept on offering.
The sun rose and sank.

The hills turned from green
to purple, to blue.

The gladioli smiled.
He wouldn't take no

for an answer.
Take no, I pleaded.

We'll go round the ring road,
he said. Give me your bag.

So I opened the grey metal carapace
of his Volkswagen Golf.

And he'd gone.

The inside was red-ribbed,
airless and hollow.

I sat there with my will,
my watery will.

Nothing else for company.
Just the bolting forwards –

and a neighing
heard through water.

EUROPA AND THE BULL

I

The herd was slipping down the green glass hill.
Twenty heifers and a bull.

A force in the sky
switched the lights off and on
to the accompaniment of a new
kind of weather, not snow, not sleet,
but the cold slanted down.
                              Although
it was Spring it was treacherous
for the heifers and the bull – they were glad
when the sky was swept clear.

II

Someone or something was driving
them down to the shore.
                              The sand
stretched out like the floor
of the world – and the sea
rushed up to it, telling
a bit of its story
                    and snatching it back.

The cows kept on paddling.
The sun was faint and then strong.

III

Europa was very much the King's daughter –
    his eyes, his nose,
and sometimes she felt she wore
his heavy gold crown, that his
kingdom trailed behind her like a dress.
She was glad to be outdoors, running
with friends along the open shore,
throwing the ball of conversation
high into the air – it spun
         backwards and forwards –
the girls swapped all the wisdom
they had gained so far.

IV

Her friends were there –
               Then they'd gone,

spirited away like a childhood.
She wrapped their voices
around her, tucked them under her arm.
Aloneness – like a thistle on her tongue.

V

She was softening, melting,
collapsing onto the sand.
And a beast was stepping towards her
dragging the sea behind him –
light in step as a dancer,

white as a boulder,
a snowy mountain,
a ship's sail,
a lie.
Orchid-white,
violet-white,
rose-white,
not white at all.

A bull blessed with the costliest
golden horns, each gleaming
to outshine the other.

VI

His tender glance
settled on her,
flitted on and off
like a cabbage-white.

Europa stretched out her hand
and touched him
                    and the being
who hid like a stowaway
inside him.

VII

He cavorted on the shore
for her pleasure and his own.
The two joys wound together.
He rocked on his back on the sand
open to her gaze, and to the sky.

She picked

    sea-blite
    sea-purslane
    glasswort
    saltwort

wove him a stiff bluish garland,
threaded it around his horns,
fed him a sea-crocus.

VIII

Fired by her boldness, he
offered her the great white cliff
of his breast to stroke.

Dear bull. Her human words
encircled him like freed birds,
alighted on his head,

fluttered into his watchfulness,
his wordless sympathy.

His huge absent bellow.

IX

And she kissed the expanse of forehead,

a kiss she feared
would make no impact,
like a tiny coin
dropped on a vast plain.

She kissed the silver line of his silence.

X

Climb onto his back,
the air seemed to say.
Cling to his broad white neck.

He bowed low, beckoning her
with half-knowing looks,
and she clambered up the milky hill of him
until they were one –

Europa and the bull, motionless
for an instant, answerable
to the sea and sky.

XI

She held on to him as she had often
held on to a stone,
or a leaf torn from a privet hedge,

fastened herself to his neck –
her floating branch,
or life itself,
                there to be grasped.

XII

He carried her along at the sea's edge,
carefully, at first,
                tried to lick her arms,
her face.

Splashed her –

teasingly
                stepping into the waves

XIII

and back again.

        Then forward

plunging in

        and plung-

ing in

       repeatedly

this was no game

deeper

       deeper

harder

       without pause

harderharder

until there was no return.

XIV

But still
        she pressed her legs
against the swimming bull,
clutched him, slid against
his heaving paleness.

Where was she,
Agenor's daughter?
Wrenched from herself,
flung across worlds.

XV

For miles
        she slithered,
torn and bleeding
on her shifting white rock.

The bold waves drowned
her cries, forced her under.

*

Then even they lay low.
The exhausted winds died down.

XVI

Beyond all hope –
                a shoreline,

calm waves, weak sun.

*

The bull knelt,
lowered his prize down

on the untrodden sand
at the blurred brink of the Earth.

XVII

Europa tumbled from his back,
her life reduced
                to a terrible soreness.

Her body, that precious thing
she'd tried to look after –

as if it were a kitten
that had grown up with her.

Her bones cried out.
Her muscles wept.

XVIII

Struggling up, she saw
a bull's shape
near to her, then further off.

She called to her friends.

Her father.

No answer –

XIX

but a slight breeze,
danced on the waves – then faster,
whipping round the distant bull

the hilly outline shook
and gleamed
            dazzled
and shook
            and a man stepped through

an empty shining frame,
                    tall and bronzed
as if the beach, or the sun had given birth.

And where was the bull?
The golden horns flashed for a moment
above the human curls.

XX

I am Jupiter, lord of all bulls,
King of the gods,

and you, Europa, a continent
full of undiscovered countries.

His eyes roved,
wandered her borderless fields,
her towns, her woods.

His face softened,
and even as she trembled
he drew her in.

She was already his queen.

XXI

A palace up a thousand steps, roofed
in mist – the birds flocked in.

Halls, courtyards teemed
with half-people, half-animals, beings in flux.
Words broadened into barks and bleats.

Visitors were clouds massing
damply at the doors.

XXII

Coming to, awake beside her gentle king
she felt his skin
                    odd to touch
like soft white suede
and saw instead of Jupiter, a bull.
And she turned and scrambled
from a bed
            churning, wide as the sea.

Europa, forgive me.
Her immortal lover bowed his head,

and cried.

XXIII

Darkness fought off the daylight
and Europa fought off the dark.

Rooms drawn in charcoal.

She hadn't known there were
so many
        shades of black.

In every corridor
visitations – of herself
                    sliding
from a wet bull,
smashed under,
            drowning,

clambering up
and drowning.

Thoughts hammering,
intruding upon her
                like strangers

breaking into her bedroom.

The sleep-grabber
at work all night,
                pulling her
with a rough hand
from a sleep
shallow as a puddle.

Europa haunted by Europa.
Her ravaged twin,
scratched as a pane of glass.

XXIV

Through screens, through limpid water,
she'd watch him
changing for the hell of it.

He'd sprawl, a leopard on a branch,
languid, ominous.

*

A mile long snake, he'd spiral up a tree.

*

Sometimes her hair
                                    flew
across her face
with nothing to blow it.

*

Or a finger
                        rippled outwards
like a stream.

*

Or her whole body
strained and cracked, and spread.

XXV

Until – stopping at a gilded mirror
                          she gazed

at a continent, a home to countries,

ripening fields, orchards, valleys,
placid lakes, mountains, plains and seas,
saw a girl and a friendly bull
                            playing on a shore,

the ocean tumult, the wilderness,
                            a father
tearful in his palace.

Her lands stirred, her rivers ran on.
Can we forgive him?
Their song.

Night

(after Jules Supervielle)

The night outside me
and the night within
dare to mingle their stars.
And I row swiftly on
between these familiar
darknesses, then pause
to take everything in.
It's a shock
to see myself from afar –
a frail speck
beating quickly, breathing
on deep lake water.
Night runs its hands
down my sides.
But which night is it?
There's only one darkness
turning like a carousel
in the sky, in my veins.
It's a long time
since I disappeared.
I can see my wake
hung with stars.
It was such hard work.

The Trees Outside My Window

(after Jules Supervielle)

I'm thankful to the trees outside my window.
Only they can reach into the depth of me.
Without them, I should have died long ago –
they keep my heart alive, its eager ways.

In the long willow branches, the dark cypress,
my own ghost hides, stares out at me,
knowing me so well, pitying me in this world.
So little understanding why I stay and stay.

War and Peace on Earth

(after Jules Supervielle)

The enemy grabbed all the masks and disguised himself
　　as anything he liked.
The lovely day, the harvest, a bunch of roses
　　suddenly went mad, exploded, bit you to death.
So many of us died that the crowds thronged below the earth
　　rather than above it.
Towns and villages knew they would turn into corpses
　　with the speed that a living soul becomes a dead one.
The churches, which the rough hands of the centuries
　　had caressed so often,
　　fell to the ground suddenly as if in an epileptic fit –
　　to rise again as dust on the wind.
The oaks, in their great antiquity,
　　took to the air like a flight of swallows.
The war turned priceless jewels to dry powder
　　causing everyone to cough and spit blood.
All those in possession of a body
　　felt it turning to fog.
And each one tasted his own ashes in his mouth.
But one day people whispered to each other
　　Peace has come.
And that seemed so strange they no longer recognised
　　their own voices.
Then the murmur repeated itself over and over,
　　beating the air awkwardly
　　like doves' wings flapping.
Under all the layers of suffering the word 'victory'
　　had disappeared from the language.
Gradually the whole earth, still freshly turned over
　　by death and the wounded
　　began to sing 'Peace has come' in a hoarse voice.
The cart found its wheels again and the horse its forelegs
　　and hind legs for galloping.
The trees found their deeply buried roots, and their sap,
　　no longer terrorised, started to flow
　　to the furthest twigs.

The church checked its steeple, right to the tip,
    and its foundations stopped debating their chances
    of survival in the bedrock.
The sheep in the meadow disappeared into their wool
    and their profound dullness
    as they'd done throughout time,
And the cows once again gave milk fresh as the new peace.
Life is put back into the people like a sword into a sheath.
Blood no longer seeks out blood
    in a neighbour's stomach,
The enemy's face stops gleaming up close
    like an instrument of torture
    with the gift of speech,
The cantata 'Peace has come' echoes round the earth
And the war dead, so as not to be late for
    the humble public holiday
Race down the endless stairs
Rushing, slipping, falling
In a great silent tumult.
All those cheated of their lives
    gesticulating and grumbling,
    commandeering a place among us
    as quickly as they can
So they can see, with eyes still able to see,
The faces of the living when at last peace returns to
    the earth.

I Hold My Breath in This Country with Its Sad Past

I hold my breath for fear of saying the wrong thing.

I hold my breath in admiration.

Because everything points to this hinterland –
the generosity of the people
the rawness of the cold
the over-heated rooms
the scooped-out cottage-loaf filled with soup.

And sometimes all talk seems delicately
configured around a silence.

I can't begin to imagine how a whole people
could be so cruelly punished.

Slowly, slowly the present
slips through the hands of the past.
And at the flick of a switch

it is red and not grey that I see
beneath the thin layer of snow.

Up the main street, under the Christmas lights
stalk the wolves, lynxes and brown bears
of the forests, and even they
have thoughts, sorrow and pride.

The Crossing

God, or someone, had parted the sea, and who were we
to say we weren't going to walk through it?

The cliff-like corridor, its glassy walls. We didn't dare
speak in case the great lift-doors of the earth would close

and drown us – feared to touch the translucent sides,
shells and seaweed fixed to a screen.

Fish stared, large as cabins, small as fingernails:
the knife-like, the black funereal, the bridal-tailed.

We moved as one, as surely as if we'd sponsored
each other. And those of us at war with ourselves,

our different parts were fused together.
We were twinned with our own undulating faces.

Who could know how our dire and honourable world
would re-establish itself?

The sky was below us and the sand above us.
Bitter as chocolate, the east wind blew all night.

Hanging

Like a raindrop suspended from a twig,
or the flower on the brink

of saying goodbye to its stalk,
history is hanging,

along with the tyrant
and the woman who murdered her lover.

The countries adhere to the globe – just.

And the day is ratcheted
along all the stages of a crisis.

A day is not a compact thing.
Necks are bullish and vulnerable.

The boulders and the dust-motes.
Hang them.

The sun blinks and blinks
with grit in its eye.

As a child, I picked up my pen
and marvelled

how the ink clung in the nib,
the tiny miracle.

Sunday

The peace treaty
is hiding in the darkness
like a grown-up
not wishing to be found.

Such an agreement is
out of this world.
Dogs might sniff at it.
It's a cold fish on a plate.

Bad news is brisk.
There's advantage in decay.
A lifetime ago.
A lifetime from now.

Someone's left behind,
or pushed in front.
The breathing of the streets
is extinguished.

The afternoon is upside-down
reflected in a pool.
We wake at night
to the pollen of what we said.

Honour

Brothers
        with knives

and my long silk scarf
from the High Street, Little India.

Brothers
        closing the flimsy curtains.

The chairs in their usual place.
The ornaments on the mantelpiece.

But it could have been
a forest clearing,
the animals scurrying away.

Brothers,
        older brothers

lunging at me
with the knife used for dicing lamb,

twisting and tightening
my own silk scarf,

the gold running through it
like waves in a violet sea.

Mother stood by like a statue.
Grandmother, sent away.

Father,
        mother,
                brothers,

I had believed each one of you
capable of kindness
in that dim front-room.

I am there, and I am missing.
As is God.

The Veil

We thought we knew the sky
spread out above us.
But now it too is veiled.

We read newspapers through a haze.
The rose wears a veil though
it cannot shield us from its thorns.

What is the veil but a kind of partition,
light as gossamer,
or dark as the River Styx?

Behind it eggs are cracked open
and the yolks run everywhere.
All we'd ever wanted to see

flickers across its window –
a boulevard, a skating rink.
Novelty, gorgeousness, lament.

The veil with its hidden waist and hips,
its energies, its limitations.
The capacious veiled veil.

The world itself is veiled.
The receding east, the receding west.

To My Posthumous Self

(after Jules Supervielle)

You died from love of the world,
that terminal illness.

Here you are lying under the turf,
not a marble headstone
but the simple summer grass.

And the bees fly past.
They say that all has turned out well
and that you're here, dead...

Those strange gentlemen, the funeral Shades
guided you with their sure hands,
their dirty fingernails –

and that was how they erased you
from that perpetual line,
the human race.

At last you sleep, never
to awaken, horizontal
but with no horizon.

Undesirable, and desiring nobody.
Sound asleep. But oh,
to make a ripple,
a little circle in a lake.

Fish Swimming

(after Jules Supervielle)

Fish swimming in the deep-water coves –
I can do nothing with your slow recollections.
Hints of foam and shadow, that's all I know of you,
and that one day, like me, you must die.

So why do you come to peer into my dreams
as if I could be of some help to you?
Swim out to sea, leave me on dry land.
We weren't meant to mix up our lives.

In the Forest

(after Jules Supervielle)

In the forest beyond time
a tall tree is cut down.
A lofty emptiness trembles
like a wound
near the horizontal trunk.

Fly this way, birds
and build your nests here
in this memory of height. Quickly,
while it is still murmuring.

Red Apples

After sleep has escaped you
night after night
someone will say that you look very well.

It's because your cheeks glow
like red apples

from Samuel Palmer's visionary tree.

They're so good, so deceptively good
it's a pity
you can't reach up to your face
and pluck them.

Like the queen in Snow White,
offer them with a smile.

Europa's Dream

She lay on a smooth white floor,
a bull-man squatting between her legs.

With the greatest attention he drew
all he saw – every soft red detail.

He couldn't stop drawing.
He drew her hidden uterus, ovaries.

No girl he said *deserves a secret.*

His pencil made intricate movements,
his horns scraped the air.

He moved backwards.

There were ten of him –
strapping bull-men, drawing on the floor.

Island

If I could turn myself into anything,
it would be the long green island
of my dream last night, sequestered,
uninhabited. Forest-hearts and oblongs

falling into glades of emerald, lime.
Coves and harbours, stunning heights.
And from this vantage point, I'd dream –
of what it might be like to be human.

Outsider Art

A woman with a blindfolded nose
holds a woman with a slit for a mouth.

*

A man segmented like an anatomical chart,
a pavement, the shell of a tortoise.

*

Unpublished books of hair, string, leaves,
seasoned and cooked in the oven.

*

An Eiffel Tower of rough timber and nails,
upside-down cows.

*

Her face looks one way, her eyes another.
Her cheeks rucked like a landscape.

*

Lightly shaded,
a simple door, two panels, a key in the lock.

*

A surface covered and covered and covered,
scrolled and scribbled all over.

*

Brooding gargoyles in torn scraps of fabric,
dyed arms outstretched.

*

Hundreds kneeling without any knees.
Heads, just heads. Sparrows and snowfall.

A Gift

Nothing alarming or remarkable.
Nothing to report.

I would like to speak up
for the forgettable day.

No fish to break its surface.
All calm in its mottled depths –

except for the clock's heartbeat
and an indistinct earthly hum.

The past lollops along
and the future scuttles into the distance.

Give me in its parcel of hours
a slippery, silken forgettable day.

Intimation

Between the v of your fingers in wintertime
a snowdrop hangs its tiny soundless bell.

Happiness

Halfway down the stairs
I hugged it to my chest.

It was the size of a small
collection of laundry,

the shape of the bundle
Dick Whittington carried

on a stick at his back,
or the tiny parcel of spices

(the woody ones)
my mother would lower

for the duration
into a pot of steaming pullao rice.

For the duration.
That would be a fine thing.

Upholding the 'I'

I try to uphold the 'I'
to push it upright

the clear, straight 'I'
stalking onwards

or resting on its back
the horizontal 'I'
like a log across a stream

the 'I' leaning to one side,
aslant in the afternoon sun,

the best time for photographs.

*

The naked 'I' in an unused room
tall enough to peer out of the window.

The 'I' shouts for clothes
for a cloak to trail on the lakeside turf
for padded shoulders.

The 'I' has strange proportions.

*

'We' are its cousins,
its close confederates.

The 'I' crashes around,
trying to find its own way.

But what could be called 'its own' –
the arrows it shoots in the dark?

*

The 'I' is gold dust –
a crocus in the mouth

a smear of mustard
the bellow of the sun.

*

The 'I'.

No point hammering it
like a stake into the ground

or planting it in a dream
or digging it up –

*

the crooked 'I'

the 'I' that's bee-like, drawn to purple

the 'I' with its walk-on part

its cool green stem

Not Exactly

You've had a hard life?
Hard, yet not so hard
that you couldn't press your fingers
into it and leave an impression.

And can a life be *had*?
Not exactly. No more than
a Casanova might boast
of having had a woman.

King Agenor

Europa, my dearest daughter,
the stories you've told me –
and those you've left out.

The beach unfurling like a flower.
Your wondrous bull-prince,
all the whites of the paint-palette.

The garland you wove for his neck...
Then there's silence. Your lips move
but I hear waves, or nothing,

the air thickening and darkening.
I have never known such air,
the combustion – the delight, the dread.

Clouds no golden horn could pierce.
And that distant, stranger shore,
so closely related to this one.

And how you reached there.
And how, from afar, you saw my tears,
the hot sea I wept,

but were helpless to come to me
until now. And you tell me you are not
as you were. Not at all.

I prepared a welcome.
Opened the palace gate, set my soul
outside like a leaf on the grass.

You are larger than you were, for sure.
I am an old man.
I cannot stand back far enough to see you.